John Whitacre
October 10, 2014

Blue Jeans

Publishing Director: Laura Bamford
Executive Editor: Mike Evans
Assistant Editor: Humaira Husain
Production Controller: Melanie Frantz
Picture Research: Liz Fowler
Art Director: Keith Martin
Senior Designer: Geoff Borin
Design: Geoff Fennell

Consultant Editor: Emily Evans

First published in 1997 by **Hamlyn**,
    an imprint of Reed Consumer Books Limited,
Michelin House,   81 Fulham Road,
    London SW3 GRB
and Auckland, **Melbourne**, Singapore and Toronto

Copyright Ⓒ 1997
    Reed International Books Limited

A Catalogue record for this book is available from the British Library
iSBN 0 600 59112 3

Printed and bound in China

CONTENTS

the birth of the blues

The origin of the word 'jeans' goes back more than four hundred years to 1567, the earliest record of its use being as *'Genoese'* or *'Gênes'*, the French spelling for the italian port of Genoa, where the merchant sailors wore sturdy work pants.

Serge de Nîmes, the fabric named after the French city of Nîmes from where it originated, became known as 'denim'.

A German chemist, Adolf von Baeyer, developed the first synthetic indigo dye in 1878, and soon after blue jeans were born.

FORTYNINERS

gold fever

Through the 19th Century, the population of the United States rocketed from four million to over sixty million, and for most of those immigrants it represented a land of hope and promise where dreams of a better life would come true.

The promise was made even more real with the California Gold Rush of 1849, and the '49ers' – the gold prospectors – needed strong and inexpensive workwear to help them realise those dreams.

Levi Strauss and Co was founded in 1850, by 1855 manufacturing Waist High Overalls and 'pantaloons' for the new mining community, using the duck and sail cloth they had originally intended for use on tents and covered wagons.

~the miner
former mechanic and cattle raiser all over the west prefer

cut full – honestly made –

Levi Strauss & Co's. copper riveted **Overalls**

the most persistently advertised – the best selling brand. it will pay you to handle

BLUE EYES MINE

in 1860 the Strauss company began making the overalls in 9oz. *serge de Nîmes,* which was supplied by the Amoskeag Manufacturing Company of New Hampshire.

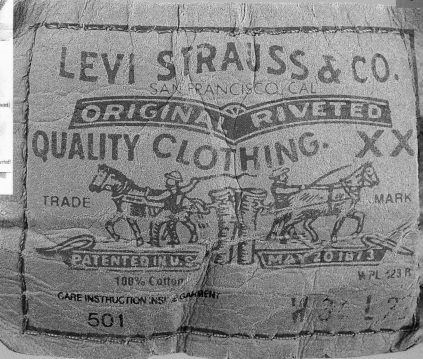

in 1873 Levi Strauss and Co. and Jacob Davis jointly patented the latter's invention of metal rivets being utilised to reinforce the stress points in the overalls.

After a publicity stunt which involved two horses trying unsuccessfully to pull apart a pair of jeans, LS&Co introduced their leather patch with the two-horse symbol in 1886.

The HD Lee Mercantile
Company, which was
founded in 1889, began
producing the Lee Bib
Overall in 1911, and in
1913 devised a garment
combining a jacket and
bib overalls called the
Lee Union-All, staple
wear for American
manual workers for
the next thirty years.

During the First World War, women having to work in the factories found themselves in denim for the first time.

For EVERY FIGHTER & WOMAN WORKER

UNITED WAR WORK CAMPAIGN

CARE for HER through The YWCA

'heigh-ho, heigh-ho. . .'

As America expanded, industry exploded. By the end of the 19th Century 170,000 miles of rail track was supported by an industrial base that included everything from coal mines to steel mills to engineering factories. Before the 1920s, HD Lee concentrated mainly on industrial wear, in particular for railroad workers, in the same way that Levi Strauss did for the mining industry.

modern times

During the 1920s, the automobile was king. Ford's factories in Detroit were challenged by General Motors and Chrysler, and there were 26 million vehicles on America's roads by 1929. Likewise, all manufacturing industry boomed, supplying a consumer demand never before seen in history. And construction was unprecedented, outwards and upwards, from the spread of the modern suburb to the ascencion of the skyscraper. The United States of America was the mightiest industrial nation on earth, and blue jeans were the uniform of the American working man.

Ripley's *Believe it Or Not!* syndicated newspaper feature teamed up with HD Lee in this clever piece of promotion from 1938.

Charlie Chaplin in denim? Unlikely, but it happened (right) in his famous 1936 satire on the industrial workstyle *Modern Times*.

the great depression

When the Great Crash of 1929 decimated industry, and the drought that turned the world's breadbasket into the midwest Dustbowl similarly scoured the agricultural community, for millions of industrial workers and farm folk destitute in Depression America denims became the basic in hard-wearing economy clothing.

Henry Fonda (right) represented the dignity of the working man preserved in denim bib and brace in the movie version of John Steinbeck's Dustbowl epic *The Grapes of Wrath*.

COWBOYS

The top rodeo stars wear

BLUE BELL

Wranglers
the authentic Western jeans

GERALD ROBERTS, WORLD'S CHAMPION ALL-AROUND COWBOY

Another Top Rodeo Star Who Wears Wranglers

Hard-riding ranch hands—top rodeo stars—men and boys everywhere wear Wranglers . . . the cowboy jeans that take the toughest wear you can give them. Wranglers are cut from 11-oz. heavy-duty denim. They're double-stitched and reinforced with no-scratch copper rivets. They're Sanforized—fit right from the start. Styled by Rodeo Ben, tailor to top rodeo stars! At stores everywhere: men's sizes, about $3.25; youths', about $2.95; boys', about $2.49.

LEFT, BELOW: Glenn Pruitt, of Yelm, Wash. World's Champion Saddle Bronc Rider. RIGHT, BELOW: Sonny Lavender, Halliday, Texas. Bull Riding winner of Madison Square Garden Rodeo. Both wear and endorse Wranglers.

Buy BLUE BELLS when you buy: Wrangler western jeans, dungarees, blue jeans, bib over-alls, chambray and covert shirts, sport shirts, matched sets, blanket-lined jackets, coveralls, work pants. BLUE BELL, INC.—New York, Dallas, Los Angeles.

WORLD'S LARGEST PRODUCER OF WORK CLOTHES

HOW THE WEST WAS WORN

Even though most of the Hollywood cowboys who established the West as a dress style in the 30's and 40's didn't always wear jeans on screen, in real life this most American of workwear was *de rigueur* for farmers, farmhands and the disappearing breed of real cowboys who worked the cattle trails across Wyoming, Nebraska, Oklahoma and down into Texas.

Although the industrial application of early jeans — in the case of Levi's targeted particularly at the gold mining community — was a major selling point, right from the start they also drew on associations with the Wild West in their advertising.

The Blue Bell company — which included Casey Jones, another pioneering jeans manufacturer since the turn of the century — launched its Wrangler line in 1947, although the name had been used on odd items since the '30s, emphasising once again the association with rodeos, rough riders and the American West. As the men became mere legend, the horse-handlers on Levi's label were a lasting reminder of the blue jeans' connotations with the land and open spaces. From the Dustbowl dramas of the Depression to the modern myth of Marlboro Country, the lone individual sillhouetted against the big sky of the praires, as the personification of a vanishing America, was usually denim-clad.

a red hot brand!
Wrangler western wear
by Blue Bell

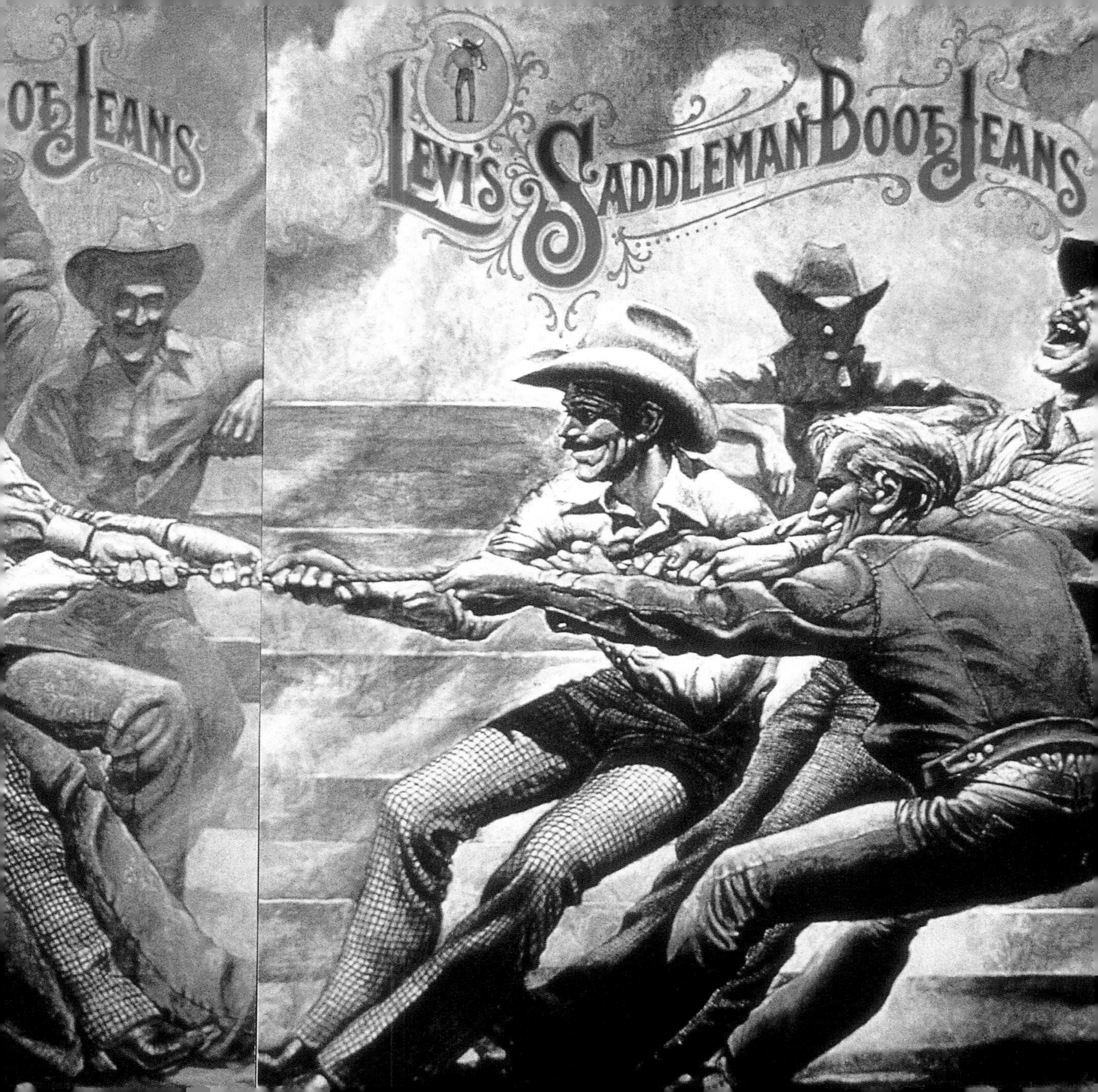
OT JEANS
LEVI'S SADDLEMAN BOOT JEANS

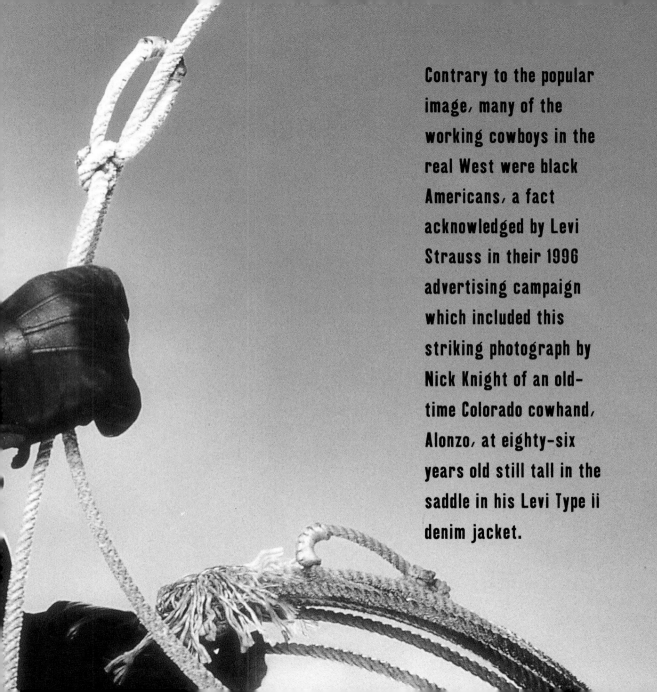

Contrary to the popular image, many of the working cowboys in the real West were black Americans, a fact acknowledged by Levi Strauss in their 1996 advertising campaign which included this striking photograph by Nick Knight of an old-time Colorado cowhand, Alonzo, at eighty-six years old still tall in the saddle in his Levi Type ii denim jacket.

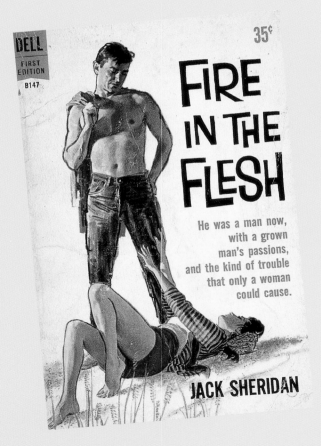

DELL

FIRST
EDITION

B147

35¢

FIRE IN THE FLESH

He was a man now,
with a grown
man's passions,
and the kind of trouble
that only a woman
could cause.

JACK SHERIDAN

Teen scene

Blue jean bop

The teenage revolution started right after the war in America, infact before teenagers were invented! They were the bobbysoxers, the kids who jitterbugged and jived to the swinging big bands of Artie Shaw and Harry James, and swooned as Frank Sinatra, Dick Haymes and Billy Eckstine crooned. It was the girls who wore the ankle-high bobby socks, which were as suited to pants as they were to pegged or flared skirts, and very soon blue jeans were to become the first truly unisex item in mass market fashion.

'There was a streetcar from San Diego by then, but the town was still quiet – too quiet. Not hardly anybody got born here. Child-bearing was thought kind of too sexy. But the war changed all that. Now we got guys that sweat, and tough school kids in Levi's and dirty shirts..'
Raymond Chandler, Playback.

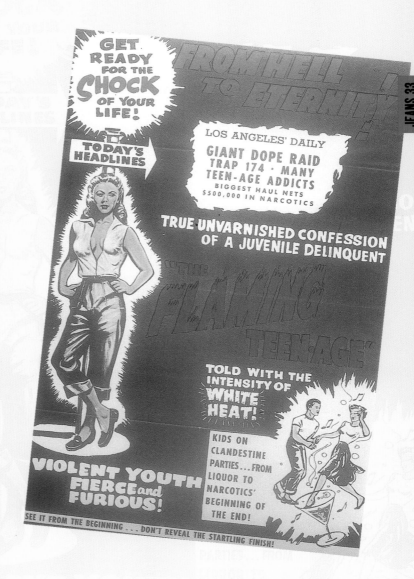

New kids on the block

During the Fifties the Blue Bell Company, home of Wranglers, began to diversify into the youth and children's market with lines that included 'Jeanies' for girls, Walt Disney character Play-Wear, and what were reputed to be the first black denim jeans, made for the tv and movie cowboy star Hopalong Cassidy and then marketed as 'Hoppys'.

● RUGGED
Lee RIDers
score in the schoolyard!

Driving in for a lay-up or going up for a rebound, Lee Riders are built for action…and made to take it! They're shaped better so they fit better. They hug the legs and cling to your back. They look rugged and they are rugged—the toughest denim ever built into "Go" Clothes. No-scratch rivets! Sanforized! Satisfaction guaranteed with these authentic cowboy jeans or your money back, or a new garment free!

Leesures by Lee

The H. D. Lee Company, Inc., Kansas City, Mo.—©1959.

Lady's Wranglers were introduced in 1949. Initially they had a zip fastener at the front, just like the men's, but this wasn't popular at first so it was moved to a side fastening, until later it became accepted to have a front fly.

THE STORY OF A TEEN-AGE FIRE-BOMB!

LOOK OUT! SHE'S SET TO EXPLODE!

"the Green-eyed Blonde"

JEANS 35

She dates her guys through a barbed wire fence!

IT'S SHAMEFUL BUT IT'S REAL!—THE NAKED TRUTH TOLD BY A GIRL WHO LIVED IN A HOME FOR UNWED MOTHERS!

GIRLS ON A RUMBLE! Scratch, bite, anything goes when you're fighting for a guy!

Untamed Youth

Juvenile delinquency was a very fashionable trend during the 1950s, among those who preached against it as well as those who practised it. There were pulp novels devoted to it, teen-movies celebrating it (often with the marvellous Mamie Van Doren, seen above in *Untamed Youth*) and newspaper crusades against it. And all this miscreant youth, it seemed, wore jeans.

Once girls were wearing the trousers, there was no limit to the lengths they would go to get their own way. *The Violent Years* (below) and *Blue Denim* were typical teen-epics appealing to youthful cinema-goers.

the lost innocence... the rude awakening to what they had done...

ARTHUR (AGE 18):

"You're not going to go anywhere —or do anything. I'm ~~re~~sponsible and I know ~~a~~ way out.. I'll take care of everything..."

MARSHA HUNT

CinemaScope

20. Century-Fox

JAMES DEAN,
the most enduring teen icon of all, only made three movies, blue jeans playing a major role in them all. There was Cal Trask and tyrannical father in *East of Eden*, Jett Rink sprawled across the cinemascopic poster for *Giant*, and the ultimate misunderstood teenager Jim Stark in *Rebel Without a Cause*.

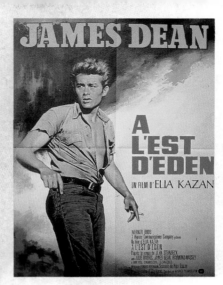

JEANS 42

steppin' out in the Seventies

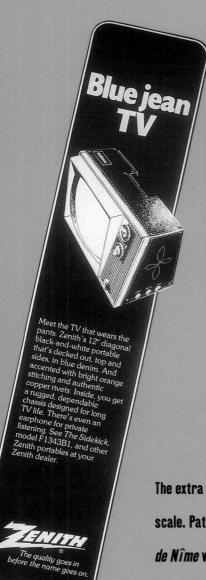
The extra denim on flares encouraged customising on an hitherto unprecedented scale. Patches, fringes, badges and other additions to the classic texture of *serge de Nîme* were given a whole new area of influence below the knee, on pants that made that other Seventies phenomenon - platform shoes– visually redundant.

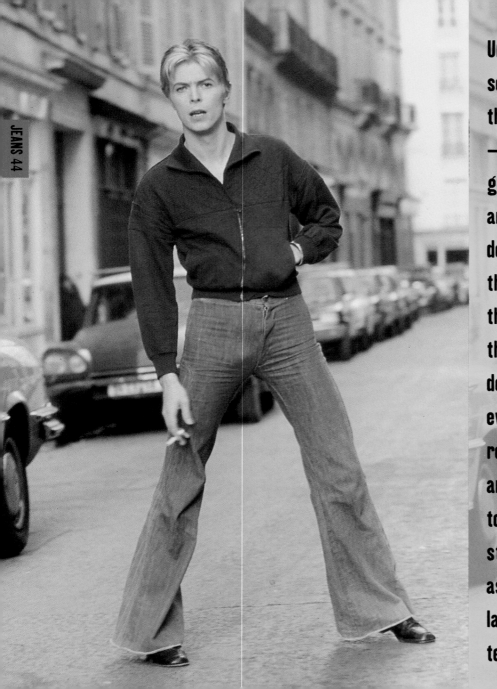

Until they enjoyed something of a revival in the mid '90s, flared jeans – along with flared pants generally – provoked an amazing amount of derision from the moment they went out of fashion in the mid 1970s. Yet through the first half of that decade flares, and their even more exaggerated relations bell-bottoms and loons, were *the* way to wear denim, for pop stars and fashion models as well as the more often lampooned footballers and television celebrities.

REBEL REBEL!

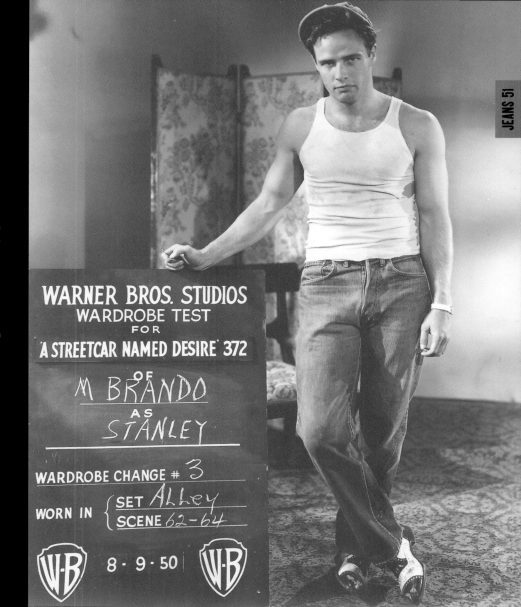

'Dean was still wearing washed-out tight Levi's and a T-shirt and looked suddenly like a real Denver character again'
Jack Kerouac,
On The Road

WARNER BROS. STUDIOS
WARDROBE TEST
FOR
'A STREETCAR NAMED DESIRE' 372
OF
M BRANDO
AS
STANLEY

WARDROBE CHANGE # 3
WORN IN { SET ALLEY
           SCENE 62-64

W-B   8·9·50   W-B

London squatters (below), Amsterdam hippies (right) and anarchist protesters in italy (opposite) all making their point

Whether in rural hippy communes, urban squats or the nomadic latter-day gypsy camps of New Age travellers, the voluntarily displaced, dispossessed and usually disgruntled are usually to be found in a rag tag array of definitely non-designer denim.

ROAD MOVIE REBELS

Woody Harrelson and Juliette Lewis,
Natural Born Killers

Martin Sheen, *Badlands*

in the true spirit
of *On The Road,* road
movie rebels from
Two Lane Blacktop to
Thelma and Louise
(left) were modern
day pioneers of the
great open spaces of
the West, and, as
did their mythical
predecessors, hit
that lonely highway
in blue jeans.

WOODSTOCK NATION

'Acres and acres of blue denim' was how more than one paper described the great rock festivals of the late Sixties and early Seventies, when a whole generation flocked to Monterey, Woodstock and the isle of Wight to get it on with nature, music and each other. And when the rains came – which they seemed to more often than not – the fans were usually more washed out than their jeans.

JEANS 57

Smarty Pants

The Calvin Klein campaign featuring model Patti Hansen (previous page) in 1979, was one of the first real designer inroads into the previously mass market territory of denim jeans, and in the 1980s 'casuals', for instance among UK football fans, popularised designer jeans like Armani and Valentino. Also on the street brief trends included stretch jeans, stripes and piping on jeans, stone wash and marble wash jeans.

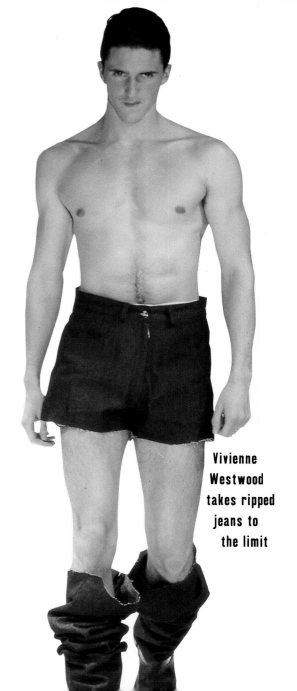

Vivienne Westwood takes ripped jeans to the limit

Patches
for poseurs,
Alexander
McQueen,
1996

Black
is back:
Christian
Lacroix,
1993

Distressed
Westwood
'91

Naomi
Campbell
in Versace,
1992

Throughout the Eighties and Nineties almost everyone in the world of high fashion, from Jean-Paul Gaultier to Vivienne Westwood and Paul Smith to Katharine Hamnett, seemed to plunder the pioneers for inspiration, but in the case of blue jeans classic is definitely not couture, and in a move back to basics the design of the original is now worn and recognised as both the essential and the best.

Schiffer
in Chanel

ACKNOWLEDGEMENTS

The publishers would like to thank the following agencies and photographers for supplying illustrative material for use in this book. We are particularly grateful to Lee Apparel Ltd, Levi Strauss Ltd, Wrangler Ltd and David Hillman from Pentagram Design Ltd for their kind co-operation with our project.

ADVERTISING ARCHIVES/Lee Apparel Ltd 14, 15, 16, 16 inset, 34 right,/Levi Strauss Ltd 26/27,/Charles Tracy c/o Staley-Wise Gallery, N.Y.,/Calvin Klein Jeans 58/59,/Wrangler Ltd 22/23, 23 inset, 26 inset, 32 left, 40/41

AQUARIUS PICTURE LIBRARY 54, 55 top, 64,/United Artists Corporation 42,/Warner Bros 51

ARCHIVE PHOTOS/Jon Hammer 30,/Lambert 17 right, 25

CAMERA PRESS/Ron Reid 43 right

THE CONDE NAST PUBLICATIONS LTD/Vogue 17 left

CORBIS UK LTD/Bettman 10/11,/Bettman-UPi 38/39, 50, /Everett 6/7, 36/37,/Everett-Warner Bros 39 inset

RONALD GRANT ARCHIVE 55 bottom

HULTON GETTY PICTURE COLLECTION 19, 52 left, 52 right, 53, /Dorothea Lange 20

NICK KNIGHT/Levi Strauss Ltd 28/29

KOBAL COLLECTION/AiP 48/49,/Twentieth Century Fox 21

LEVI STRAUSS LTD endpapers

MAGNUM PHOTOS/Philippe Holsman bk jkt inside flap

NIALL MCINERNEY/Versace 62 left

CHRIS MOORE/Chanel 63,/Christian Lacroix 61 right, /Alexander McQueen 61 left,/Vivienne Westwood 60, 62 right

PETER NEWARK'S AMERICAN PICTURES 8, 11 right, 12, 18 background, 24/25,/Levi Strauss Ltd 13 left, 26 background

NOVA/JEAN-PAUL GOUDE 46/47

PICTORIAL PRESS 45, 56 top left

REDFERNS/Elliott Landy 56 bottom left, 56 /57

RETNA 44/45,/Holland Frnt jkt inside flap

REX FEATURES/Tim Rooke/Levi Strauss Ltd 13 right, /Frank Shorty Wilcox 2/3

SYGMA 9,/Levi Strauss Ltd 11 inset

VINTAGE MAGAZINE Co 24, 31, 33, 34 left, 43 left, /Jesus Jeans 4/5,/Lee Apparel Ltd 18 inset, 32 right, /Warner Bros 35, 38 inset